D1404391

My Favorite Machines

Submarines

Colleen Ruck

A+

Smart Apple Media

Smart Apple Media
P.O. Box 3263, Mankato, MN 56002

 An Appleseed Editions book

Planning and production by Discovery Books Limited
Designed by D.R ink
Edited by Colleen Ruck

Library of Congress Cataloging-in-Publication Data
Ruck, Colleen.
 Submarines / by Colleen Ruck.
    p. cm. -- (My favorite machines)
 Includes index.
 ISBN 978-1-59920-678-3 (library binding)
 1. Submarines (Ships)--Juvenile literature. I. Title.
 VM365.R79 2012
 623.825'7--dc22
                        2011010306

Photograph acknowledgments
BAE Systems: p. 23, Royal Navy: p. 18; Shutterstock: pp. 5 (Helmut Konrad Watson), 10 (Danilo Ducak), 13 top (Jens Stolt); U.S. Navy: pp. 4, 5, 6, 7, 8, 9, 12, 14, 15, 16, 17, 19, 20, 21, 22.

Printed in the United States of America at Corporate Graphics
In North Mankato, Minnesota

DAD0502
52011

9 8 7 6 5 4 3 2 1

Contents

What is a Submarine?

A submarine is a boat that can travel underwater. It can stay underwater for many days.

This submarine is used for **exploring** the ocean floor.

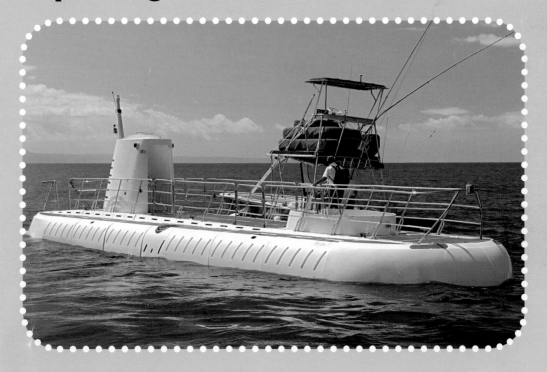

Controls

The control room is in the center of the sub. This is where the crew steer the submarine.

Sail

Plane

A sub has a sail on top. It has a **plane** on each side of the sail. The planes steer the sub upward or downward.

At Sea

This submarine is going down,
or diving. When it comes back
up again, it is surfacing.

This submarine is traveling
under the North Pole. It can
surface through thin ice.

Weapons

Attack submarines fire **weapons** called torpedoes. They travel through the water and **explode** when they hit an enemy ship.

Silo

Attack subs can also fire **missiles** into the air. The missiles are stored in tubes called **silos**.

Subs in Hiding

Submarines can be attacked by other ships or aircraft. To hide, they stay underwater most of the time.

A propeller pushes the sub along quickly, but very quietly.

This sub is powered by jets of water.

Life on a Submarine

As many as 150 people live on board a big sub. They are often cut off from the outside world.

Chefs also live on the sub.
They cook meals for the crew.

On Course

This man is a navigator.
He makes sure the submarine
stays on course.

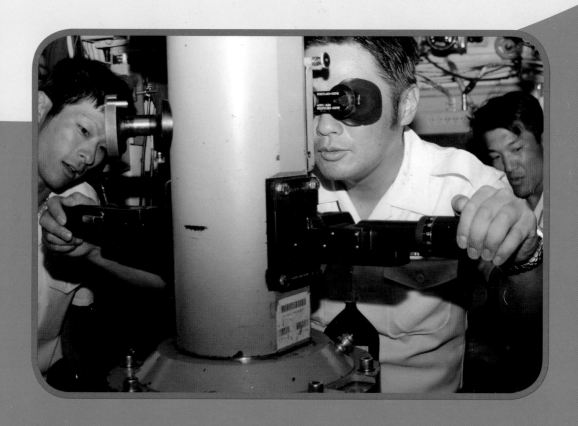

The captain uses a periscope.
This helps him to see what is
happening above the water
when the sub is underwater.

Emergency!

Rescue craft

Sometimes a sub breaks down underwater. A rescue craft is sent down to bring the crew members back to the surface.

18

This crew member is wearing a submarine escape suit. He is training for an **emergency**.

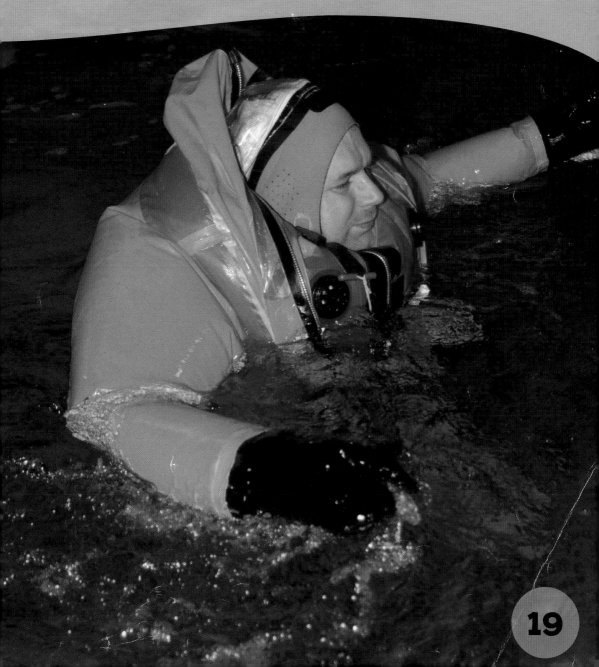

One-man Subs

Not all submarines are large
and powerful. This is a submarine
you can wear!

Some small submarines have no crew. They are controlled from the surface.

Future Submarines

In the future, attack submarines will have more weapons. The USS *Ohio* can carry and launch 154 torpedoes!

Many future subs will have
no crew at all. This tiny sub is
operated by remote control.
It is looking for **mines** which
might explode.

Glossary

emergency	An unexpected and serious event.
explode	To blow up.
explore	To travel around finding out what a place is like.
mine	A hidden bomb that explodes when something touches it.
missile	A weapon that is fired at a target.
plane	The planes on a submarine are like the wings of an aircraft. They direct the sub upward or downward.
silo	A long tube used for storing missiles.
weapon	An object used to hurt or kill people in a fight or war.

Web sites

http://www.navy.mil/navydata/fact_display.asp?cid=4100&tid=100&ct=4
Learn about the different types of submarine.

www.rnsubmus.co.uk
Look at the exhibits on view at the Royal Navy Submarine Museum in Britain.

http://science.howstuffworks.com/nuclear-submarine5.htm
Find out how a nuclear submarine works.

Index